Coming Together

with

Yourself

and Your

People

NIKKI HART

Ark House Press
arkhousepress.com

© 2025 Nikki Hart

Cataloguing in Publication Data:
Title: Coming Together With Yourself And Your People
ISBN: 978-1-7641362-6-6 (pbk)
Subjects: REL012040 RELIGION / Christian Living / Inspirational;
REL012170   RELIGION / Christian Living / Personal Memoirs;
REL012120 RELIGION / Christian Living / Spiritual Growth.
Design by initiateagency.com

❧

I gift this to every heart that needs a little light —
and especially to my babies, Gypsy and Noah.
May you always know how deeply you've inspired
me to pour more love into the world.

❧

Contents

Chapter One: To Every Heart That Feels Small 1

Chapter Two: The Ripple of Kindness 7

Chapter Three: Finding Connection When
You Feel Alone..13

Chapter Four: Exploring Your Heart and
Holding Purpose..21

Chapter Five: The Strength in Struggles........................27

Chapter Six: Talking It Out – The Power of
Conversation 35

Chapter Seven: Real Life Over Likes –
Disconnect to Reconnect.....................................41

Chapter Eight: Final Thoughts and a Prayer 47

Chapter One

To Every Heart That Feels Small

To every heart who feels small, invisible, or even just unsure of who you are and who you're meant to be — this is for you.

While my heart truly has focus to help youth and young hearts, may this resonate with anyone and everyone, especially of any age. No matter where you are on your journey — five, fifteen, thirty-five, or even eighty-five — this is a message of hope and truth. You are not alone, and you are not just a number.

I want to be real with you. Life hasn't been easy for me — it's been a mix of hardship and blessing. I didn't come to know the Lord until I was in my thirties.

Before that, I tried many paths and practices that felt right in the moment. But looking back, I can see how every experience, every joy, every pain, was leading me to discover what truly lived in my heart.

I've faced illnesses meant to break me — cancer, mental health battles, and autoimmune disease— but I didn't give in. I kept fighting, and I found that positivity, real community, and faith gave me the strength to heal and grow and keep going.

There were times I felt completely lost, unsure of who I was or where I belonged. And to be honest, I still have those days. But what's changed is the foundation I now stand on. My identity is rooted in something deeper. I've come to learn that there is always more growing, more learning, and more love to be found, and to be explored with others.

❀ ❀ ❀

1 Corinthians 16:14 - "Let all that you do be done in love."

❀ ❀ ❀

Love is powerful. So is kindness. When you lift others, you rise.

❀ ❀ ❀

Proverbs 11:25 - "A generous person will prosper; whoever refreshes others will be refreshed."

❀ ❀ ❀

Let that be the kind of power we grow in this world.

Chapter Two

The Ripple
of Kindness

Kindness is not weakness — it's one of the strongest forces we have. One small act can ripple into a wave of change. I've seen it. I've lived it.

Sometimes we're pushed to act from our own sense of justice, and that can stir up anger, pain or disappointment. It's okay to feel those things— they're part of being human. But we're not meant to be ruled by them. Instead, we're meant to use them as a way to understand what's hurting in us and how to grow through it. It can be a very useful tool for us to reflect into our lives and see what needs changing to open paths for joy.

You never know what someone else is carrying. Sometimes those who hurt us are desperate to feel heard or validated. Responding with kindness — not to excuse hurtful behavior, but to choose healing over harm — can transform hearts.

We can still hold accountability alongside kindness, and kindness is where transition happens. The kind of power kindness truly has is remarkable — by sharing a simple act of kindness, we can create echoes in places we will never even know were reached.

Share a smile, compliment someone, leave a little note of positivity for a friend to find, send a text saying, "Hey, hope you have a great day today." It can be so simple yet so powerful.

* * *

Romans 12:21 - "Do not be overcome by evil, but overcome evil with good."

* * *

* * *

Galatians 6:9 - "Let us not become weary in doing good, for at the proper time we will reap a harvest if we do not give up."

* * *

Let kindness be the legacy we leave.

Chapter Three

Finding Connection When You Feel Alone

*W*hen you feel the most alone is often when you need connection the most. And while it can be scary to reach out, it's one of the most powerful steps you can take. One of the biggest lies we're told and believe is that "if we don't fit somewhere or with someone, then we don't fit anywhere or with anyone." That's what the enemy wants us to believe — he wants that seed to grow to create doubt and division, because together is strength, together is love, and there IS a place in this world where you fit just as you are! You just need to find it!

Start with your heart. What brought you joy as a child? What made you feel most alive? What deep down brought happiness to you, especially when you were an innocent child?

Practical Tips for Reconnecting:

- ❖ Reflect on hobbies or interests you loved as a kid — drawing, soccer, dancing, playing music.

- ❖ Try doing those activities again. Your inner child will thank you.

- ❖ Explore local community events, sports groups, or art workshops.

- ❖ Invite a friend to come along with you — your invite might be exactly what they needed too.

❖ Host a potluck dinner or park BBQ. Keep it simple. Connection is about presence, not perfection.

❖ Join a book club at the library or host one at home.

❖ Volunteer for something meaningful to you — it's a beautiful way to meet like-hearted people.

❖ Go watch a sunset with a friend, or have a beach day with your favorite playlist.

❖ Say yes to the things you've put off because you were waiting to be "ready."

❖ Try new community sports, board game nights, walking groups, or local art classes.

❖ Organize a movie night under the stars or a simple Sunday coffee catch-up at a local café.

I used to hide myself away because I didn't feel "good enough." I thought my house needed to be spotless or that I had to be on top of everything. But opening up, letting people in — even when things weren't perfect — brought me the deepest connections.

And truth be told… we are all messy in some place of our lives, trust me there!

◦ ◦ ◦

Matthew 18:20 - "For where two or three gather in my name, there am I with them."

◦ ◦ ◦

Real connection heals us. And you never know who needs your presence just as much as you need theirs.

Chapter Four

Exploring Your Heart and Holding Purpose

*Y*our heart holds your purpose. That might sound big — and it is — but it doesn't mean you have to have it all figured out.

Purpose isn't always loud. Sometimes it's in the quiet persistence of showing up.

You might not know exactly what your purpose is right now, and that's okay.

Sometimes, we find it slowly — one small yes at a time. And sometimes, it changes and grows with us as we evolve.

Ways to explore your heart:

❖ Start journaling — write letters or paragraphs to yourself, to your future, or to God. Write like a diary or just get your thoughts onto paper with doodles and squiggles. It helps bring clarity.

❖ Explore your emotions without judgment. We all have emotions and feelings, and they are meant to be explored to understand what's stirring within us.

❖ Ask yourself what moments made you feel most "you." What lights you up inside? Really push into that question!

❖ Talk it out with someone safe — a friend, a mentor, a counselor. Sometimes we click with someone and sometimes we don't, and that's okay too, keep looking for the people you click with!

❖ Notice who and what brings you peace. Follow that. Always follow that!

❖ Try things — even if they're new or feel silly. Play, create, try, fail, laugh, try again. Enjoy the simple joy in trying something you've never tried before!

Remember, your purpose may not be just one thing — it may be many little things that add up to a big life filled with meaning.

· · ·

Proverbs 4:23 - "Above all else, guard your heart, for everything you do flows from it."

· · ·

Chapter Five

The Strength in Struggles

I hope these words haven't given a false portrayal that I have it all together — because let me share: I'm far from perfect. I'm messy, I'm quirky, I don't always make the right choices. I've made mistakes. And even with all my growth and self-awareness, I still have hard days. I still cry. I still wonder why.

There have been days when I felt like I was drowning in the weight of it all — sick kids, financial pressure, trying to be a good partner, a good parent, a good friend, a good person... and just feeling like I was failing at it all. There were moments I couldn't even tell you what I needed—just that I felt empty, disconnected, and exhausted. But somehow, one conversation, one prayer, one kind act from someone else reminded me that I wasn't alone. And neither are you. There is power in unity.

Struggles don't mean you're weak. Struggles mean you're human. The hardest parts of life are often where the deepest strength is formed. It's in those messy, painful places that we're shaped. It's in the reaching out, the vulnerability, the crying on someone's shoulder, or letting someone cry on yours that real healing begins, because that is where real humanity shines.

I've learned to stop expecting myself to have it all together. Instead, I've learned to show up as I am— raw, real, and ready to keep growing. Struggles are not roadblocks to your purpose — they are part of the road. And they teach us empathy, resilience, and compassion for others walking through their own storms.

Sometimes the breakthrough isn't immediate. Sometimes the strength is in simply getting up again. Other times it's in finally letting go of what's been hurting you. And often, it's in being real with someone and letting them help carry your load.

Practical reminders during hard seasons:

- ❖ Let someone in. Share what you're going through — even if it's messy or confusing.

- ❖ Don't isolate. That's what pain wants you to do, the enemy wants you all to himself, but connection is what brings healing.

- ❖ Keep a journal — write down what you're feeling, what you're learning, or just let it all out.

❖ Celebrate the small wins. Getting out of bed. Making a meal. Smiling when you didn't think you could. Even just simply having a hot shower.

❖ Lean into faith. Even if your prayers are messy or uncertain — God hears them all.

❖ Rest without guilt. Resting is not quitting. Resting is honoring your limits and allowing yourself space to recharge — like plugging in a phone when the battery is low, or filling a well that's been drawn from too many times.

You are not your struggle. You are not your failure. You are not your hardest day. You are loved, needed, and still growing. And so many others — including me — know what it feels like to battle in the quiet places.

＊　＊　＊

2 Corinthians 12:9 - "My grace is sufficient for you, for my power is made perfect in weakness."

＊　＊　＊

You don't need to be perfect to be worthy of love or connection. You just need to be open. Be real. Be you — in all the colors and baggage that includes.

Chapter Six

Talking It Out – The Power of Conversation

I used to think counseling wasn't for me — that no one could really "get" me. Though I've learned that the more I explored different supports, the more growth I found.

Sometimes we don't click with the first person we talk to, and that's okay. Not every space or support is going to feel right — and it doesn't mean there's something wrong with you. It just means you might need to keep exploring to find the people and places where you truly feel seen and understood.

Sometimes we outgrow a connection or realise it no longer serves our growth, and that's also okay. It's a reminder that your path is still unfolding, and you're meant to keep moving forward to where you belong.

Sometimes it takes a few tries to find the right person, but keep going, keep showing up for yourself:

Tips for Seeking Support:

❖ Try talking to a counselor, youth or social worker, or trusted friend.

❖ If one practitioner doesn't feel like the right fit, try someone else. We aren't designed to all click with each other; that's where the beauty in our own uniqueness shines!

❖ Group therapy or peer support groups can be powerful too.

❖ Sometimes just one deep, honest conversation with a friend or family member — even maybe a stranger — can change everything.

❖ Don't give up. You deserve support.

Growth doesn't happen in isolation — it happens in connection.

❀ ❀ ❀

James 5:16 - "Therefore confess your sins to each other and pray for each other so that you may be healed."

❀ ❀ ❀

Chapter Seven

Real Life Over Likes – Disconnect to Reconnect

*T*he digital world can be great, but when we start to rely on it for comfort or validation, it can get heavy.

I've seen in my own family how powerful it is to unplug and reconnect with each other in real life. I noticed that too much tech was leading to anxiety, irritability, and even aggression. So we purposefully disconnect — go camping, have days outside in the sun or bushwalking in the rain, fishing, adventuring, doing DIY projects together — the options are limitless! I've seen happiness and joy and laughter fill the space where negativity started to take hold. We're not meant to do life behind screens. We're meant for hugs, for laughter, for shared meals, and shoulder-to-shoulder support.

Ways to Disconnect and Reconnect:

- ❖ Schedule regular screen-free time with loved ones.

- ❖ Cook and eat meals together — invite others into that space.

- ❖ Plan potluck dinners, BBQs at the park, or beach afternoons.

- ❖ Do something creative — paint, write, build, play music with others like hearted.

- ❖ Take a walk and notice the world around you.

- ❖ Host board game nights or movie nights.

❖ Say yes to real-life moments, even if they feel small.

❖ Go to those local events and group activities!

Be purposeful in making space for connection - connection grows when we make room for it.

* * *

Hebrews 10:24-25 - "Let us consider how we may spur one another on toward love and good deeds... encouraging one another."

* * *

Chapter Eight

Final Thoughts and a Prayer

*N*ow, if you don't know Jesus or have faith or relationship there, that's okay — I hope this still sparks some positive direction for connecting and growing within your heart, life, and community - and maybe even help guide you to who you truly are in your heart.

If you're new to faith, may I encourage you to visit your local churches until you find the one that feels like home — that's your people, and they will walk it with you. You will know in your heart when you've found that place; it may take a couple of visits until you hear it, but your heart will tell you!

And to the seasoned believers, I pray this stirs something new and valuable in your own heart or maybe even highlights a person you may know who may benefit from hearing something shared here.

To bring this mini book into a wrap - who knows maybe one day the Lord will stir me to share something else, but for here and now - I'd like to share a prayer.

I pray, love and peace are felt through these words. That the Holy Spirit may come and move through this message, and in His holy might, mountains are moved and blocks that have been holding up the way toward our growth – crumble, and growing up through that rubble like a purposefully watered seed - May we seek, find and grow in connection, and purpose.

I pray for hearts to be softened, for loneliness to lift, for truth and beauty to shine through the cracks. I pray for community to find each other and for hearts to heal together. I pray people come together, celebrate, and enjoy one another. That in times where technology is so solely depended upon for comfort and valida-

tion, we are able to disconnect from the wired world and connect into each other — in real presence, real experiences, and real life. And through those connections, may true self be found.

In Jesus Name I pray, Amen

With LOVE, hope, and understanding. Blessings and thanks,

—Someone who believes in you and is walking this journey too, just like you!

♥ Nikki Hart

About the Author

Nikki is a passionate mother and heart-led encourager of kindness, connection, and faith. Her journey through illness, mental health challenges, healing, and rediscovering her identity has deeply shaped her mission to help others feel seen, heard, and valued.

"Her voice is warm, real, and full of the kind of love this world needs more of — the kind that meets people right where they are."

Nikki hopes that every reader of this mini book walks away feeling a little more connected, a little more hopeful, and a whole lot more loved.

My Happy Place

www.ingramcontent.com/pod-product-compliance
Lightning Source LLC
Chambersburg PA
CBHW031613040426
42452CB00006B/501